6171

Life in a
Swamp

Karen D. Povey

KIDHAVEN PRESS

An imprint of Thomson Gale, a part of The Thomson Corporation

THOMSON
GALE

Detroit • New York • San Francisco • San Diego • New Haven, Conn. • Waterville, Maine • London • Munich

© 2006 Thomson Gale, a part of The Thomson Corporation.

Thomson and Star Logo are trademarks and Gale and KidHaven Press are registered trademarks used herein under license.

For more information, contact
KidHaven Press
27500 Drake Rd.
Farmington Hills, MI 48331-3535
Or you can visit our Internet site at http://www.gale.com

LIBRARY OF CONGRESS CATALOGING-IN-PUBLICATION DATA

Povey, Karen D., 1962–
    Life in a swamp / by Karen D. Povey.
        p. cm. — (Ecosystems)
    Includes bibliographical references and index.
    ISBN 0-7377-3140-0 (hardcover : alk. paper)
    1. Swamp ecology—Juvenile literature. 2. Swamps—Juvenile literature. I. Title.
II. Series.
    QH541.5.S9.P68 2005
    577.68—dc22
                                                                    2005006479

Printed in the United States of America

Contents

Chapter 1

What Is a Swamp?

Wherever land and water meet, they form areas called wetlands. These wetlands may be along coasts, where the ocean meets the shore. They may be along riverbanks or along the edges of lakes and streams. They also may be in low-lying areas where water remains standing after a season of rainstorms.

Because wetlands occur in so many different places, they take many different forms. One common type of wetland is called a marsh. Marshes are places where plants such as grasses and reeds grow up out of shallow water. They are flooded with water almost all the time. Trees never grow in marshes. Instead marshes are open areas that receive a lot of sunlight.

Swamps differ from marshes in two important ways. First, many swamps do not contain water throughout the entire year. Instead, swamps hold the water that comes from a season of rainstorms. This water may dry up and disappear after the end of the rainy season. Second, trees grow in swamps. A swamp may even be thought of as a flooded forest. Just as in a forest, little sunlight reaches the ground beneath the trees in a swamp, so it is difficult for grasses and other plants to grow there.

Unlike treeless marshes, swamps support a variety of trees, such as these cypresses.

Animals interact with one another in the swamp. Here, a little blue heron snacks on a frog.

The Swamp Ecosystem

The flooded forest of a healthy swamp functions as an **ecosystem**. That means that it contains plants and animals that interact with one another to create a unique natural environment. Swamps are home to a wide diversity, or variety, of plants and animals, all of which are suited for living in their watery habitat. In North America, fish, turtles, frogs, and muskrats swim within a swamp's waters. Salamanders, snails, crabs, and shorebirds live along the edges of a swamp's pools. Raccoons, deer, opossums, and snakes prowl the higher ground within a swamp, venturing in or near the water to feed or drink.

The plants and animals that make up a swamp ecosystem vary slightly depending on where the swamp is. Swamps can be found in many different places around the world. When people think of swamps they often think of the hot and steamy wetlands of Louisiana or Florida. While the largest swamps in North America are found in the southeastern United States, swamps also can be found in climates where the temperature changes with the seasons and the winters are cold. These are called temperate swamps. The Great Swamp of New York State is one of the largest temperate swamps in the United States. If covers 6,000 acres (2,428ha) of land. This swamp is made up of deciduous trees that lose their leaves each fall, such as maples, alders, and cottonwoods. Temperate swamps such as the

Great Swamp provide a habitat for wood ducks, otters, beavers, and trout.

Most swamps, however, grow where there is little change in temperature from season to season. In the United States these places are known as the subtropics. Closer to the equator, these places are known as the tropics. These subtropical and tropical swamps, such as the Big Cypress Swamp in Florida and the Sundarbans swamp region in southern India and Bangladesh contain different groups of plants and animals than temperate swamps do. Some of the most common plants in these swamps are cypress trees, mangroves, palms, orchids, and vines.

No matter where they grow, all swamp ecosystems depend on receiving a lot of water on a regular basis. Both temperate and tropical swamps receive water in one of three ways: through the flooding of rivers, through the collection of rain, or from the ocean's changing tides.

River Swamps

Rivers are the source of water for river swamps. During the rainy season, when rains are heavy and the rivers rise, these swamps serve as floodplains that catch and store the excess water that spills from the riverbanks. A swamp, like all wetlands, occurs where the land is very flat, so the flooding water spreads out evenly over its surface. Rapidly moving floodwater from a river slows down as it flows

Water runs slowly through Cypress Creek Slough in South Carolina, creating a peaceful scene.

through the swamp, much like water flows through a sponge.

During the peak of a flood, water in the swamp may be several feet (a meter or so) deep, rising high up the trunks of the trees. When the rains stop and the river level drops, much of the water in the swamp disappears by slowly draining away downstream or evaporating in the heat of the day. It may take many months for most of the water to dry up. Even then, some water may remain in the deepest pools or lowest places in the swamp.

Some of the best-known river swamps are part of the Mississippi River system as it moves through Louisiana on its way to the Gulf of Mexico. These swamps are full of ancient cypress trees hung with drooping Spanish moss. Here, alligators make their homes. They float silently just below the surface of the water. Catfish swim in the shallows, while giant snapping turtles settle into the mud at the bottom of the swamp, waiting for an unsuspecting fish to pass close by their waiting jaws.

Stillwater Swamps

Not all swamps get their water from flooding rivers. Some swamps, known as stillwater swamps, depend on rainfall to keep them wet. These swamps are usually found in places where the land is low and flat, so rainwater collects there instead of flowing away. During the rainy season, the swamp catches and holds large amounts of water. Because it is almost always full

Tree frogs live in stillwater swamps.

of water, the soil of a stillwater swamp is very spongy. This soil drains poorly, so the water remains standing on the surface for long periods instead of sinking into the ground. These ponds are perfect hideouts for frogs and salamanders. They provide the water source these animals need to feed and lay their eggs.

Tidal Swamps

The third type of swamp is called a tidal swamp. Tidal swamps are found along the tropical and subtropical coasts of North and South America, Asia, Africa, and Australia. These swamps are home to trees called mangroves. They are also known as mangrove swamps or mangrove forests. Mangroves are one of the few land plants able to grow in the salty water at the ocean's edge.

Instead of flooding with the seasons as other swamps do, mangrove swamps have different water levels throughout the day as the ocean tides change. During the course of a single day, the twisted stalks of the mangroves may stand in several feet (1m) of water or jut directly out of the exposed mud below.

Mangroves grow best where there is a mix of freshwater and salt water. Therefore, the largest mangrove swamps grow at the mouths of rivers flowing into the sea. The largest mangrove swamp in the world is the Sundarbans of southern India and Bangladesh. This swamp covers 160 miles (260km) along the coast where the huge Ganges

Mangroves grow along the saltwater shores of tidal swamps.

River reaches its end. The swamp also extends as far as 80 miles (130km) inland in a tangle of mangrove-covered rivers, creeks, and channels. This wetland is made up of an enormous system of the flowing river and the changing tides. Here, crocodiles, monkeys, tigers, and hundreds of species of birds and fish find food and shelter within the water and mud.

Chapter 2

A Watery World

A swamp is a rich ecosystem made up of plants and animals that are able to live in lots of water. **Aquatic** animals such as fish, turtles, and alligators thrive in the waters of the swamp. For plants, the swamp is a more challenging place to live and grow. The ground in a swamp contains **hydric,** or waterlogged, soil. Because the soil is so full of water, almost no air spaces remain. That means there is little oxygen available for plants to absorb through their root systems to help them grow. Only certain plants are able to live in such a wet environment. They are known as **hydrophytic** plants and are adapted for surviving in their watery world.

Aquatic animals, such as these turtles, thrive in swamps.

Swamp Plants

A wide variety of small plants grow in the rich soil, or **sediments**, of the swamp. Each has a special way to cope with the swamp's extreme conditions. Some plants, such as pondweed and tape grass, grow entirely underwater. Some of these plants even produce flowers that are pollinated by insects under the water. Others, such as cattails, send up leaves and stalks that poke through the surface of the water. Many swamp plants, such as water lilies, produce leaves and flowers that float on the water's surface.

Other swamp plants do not put roots in the soil at all. Some plants, such as duckweed, float freely in

Plants of the Swamp

Bromeliads are air plants that grow on the surface of trees.

Milkweed produces pink flowers and can grow up to four feet high.

Water lilies are rooted in the sediment, and their leaves and flowers float on the water's surface.

Cattail is a common swamp plant found in swamps everywhere.

Duckweed grows floating freely in the water.

the water with their roots dangling. The roots absorb oxygen and nutrients directly from the water. Swamps are also home to many air plants, or **epiphytes**. Epiphytes, such as orchids and bromeliads, root directly onto the surface of tree branches instead of in the soil. Their roots gather moisture from the air and rain and receive nutrients from decaying leaves stuck among the branches.

Trees with Knees

One plant famous for its unusual root system is the cypress tree. Cypress trees have roots that grow near the surface of the soil. Here they can easily take up oxygen. Sections of a cypress tree's roots grow up out of the ground a few feet (about 1m) from the trunk. The exposed roots form knobby structures, called knees, that jut from the earth. Cypress knees tend to grow tallest, up to 5 feet (1.5m) high, where the water stands deepest. In other swamps where the water is more shallow or drains away more quickly, the knees may be only a few inches (several centimeters) tall.

Scientists are not sure of the cypress knees' function. One theory is that they allow the trees to take oxygen out of the air. It is also thought that the knees help support the trees, making them more stable in the watery ground.

Because the roots of swamp trees do not go deep into the soil and the ground is so spongy, the trees need extra support to keep them anchored. In addi-

Jutting out of the swamp, a cypress tree's knees may help support the tree in the spongy soil.

tion to the support provided by their knees, cypress trees have fin-shaped roots that grow from the wide bases of their trunks. These **buttress roots** also help prevent the trees from toppling in the soggy soil.

Roots to Breathe and Stand

The mangrove trees in tidal swamps also develop special roots for supporting their weight and absorbing oxygen. Instead of having thick knees and buttresses, mangroves have more slender roots. Just like the cypress tree, the mangrove sends out a shallow web of roots into the soil. From these roots, pencil-like stalks sprout above the surface. Called **pneumatophores**, these roots absorb oxygen during the time of the day when the tide is low and they are exposed to the air.

Some types of mangroves grow oxygen-absorbing roots from the sides of their trunks. These prop or **stilt roots** extend out from the mangrove tree like arms. They arch down, eventually growing into the mud. Over time, the mangrove grows a cluster of stilt roots that reach down from all sides of its

The mangroves' slender roots help the trees absorb oxygen and form a web of support against the changing tides.

trunk. Often mangroves will grow close together in groupings called groves. Within these groves, the trees' stilt roots intertwine to form a web of support that anchors them in the unstable mud of the changing tides.

Too Much Salt

Mangrove trees face another survival challenge not shared by plants that grow in freshwater swamps—the salty water of the ocean. Plants living in seawater draw salt up through their roots along with the water. If a plant absorbs too much salt into the tissues of its stem or leaves, it will die.

To survive in the saltwater environment of the coast, mangrove plants must keep the salt out. Their roots are their first line of defense. Mangroves' roots prevent some of the salt from being absorbed as they draw water into the tree. Salt that does enter is stored within the leaves and stems. Some types of mangroves filter out the salt, depositing salt crystals on the surface of the leaves. This salt is washed away by the rain or blown off in the wind. In some mangroves the salt remains in the leaf until it dies and falls off.

Swamp Creatures

Plants and animals able to adapt to the challenging environment of the swamp are rewarded by the nutrition the swamp's rich soil provides. Swamp soil has large amounts of nutrients from minerals and

Animals of the Swamp

Alligators are the best-known reptiles in the swamp.

Raccoons are nocturnal, so they are rarely seen during the day.

Herons feed on fish, worms, snakes, and other small animals.

Deer live along the edges of the swamp.

Beavers are aquatic animals that spend most of their time in the water.

decaying plants. This nutrient-rich sediment provides a rich layer at the bottom of the swamp and forms the foundation for the swamp food web. This sediment is eaten by snails, crabs, and shrimp. These animals, in turn, are food for the larger animals of the swamp.

The rich nutrients and complex root systems of the mangrove swamp provide an ideal habitat for wildlife. Small creatures, such as fish and shrimp, dart in the hidden spaces below the surface. Barnacles and oysters cling to the mangroves' roots. Scuttling crabs move sideways up the roots, while lizards stalk prey from above. When water recedes from the shore at low tide, wading birds, small mammals, and monkeys roam the exposed mud in search of worms, snails, fish, and crabs that have become stranded in shallow pools.

Cypress swamps also are home to a rich and varied community of animals. Spineless invertebrates such as worms, insects, crawfish, and leeches feed from the sediment and serve as food for fish and birds. Beavers, herons, and otters feed in the swamp's waters, while raccoons and deer roam the swamp's edges. Songbirds nest high in the treetops or in hollowed out cypress knees.

Alligator Holes

Some of the most common creatures in the swamp are reptiles such as snakes, lizards, and turtles. The best-known reptile in the cypress swamp is the alligator.

Alligators are fearsome predators, feeding on almost all the other animals of the swamp. Although they are a danger to most animals, alligators actually play an important role in keeping the other swamp creatures alive during times of drought.

During the dry season, much of the water in a swamp drains away or dries up. The water that remains forms pools in the deepest areas. Alligators and other aquatic animals take refuge in these pools. As algae and other plants grow and begin to fill in the pools, alligators keep them clear by using their snouts and feet to shovel the plants and muck up onto the shore. These cleared pools are known as alligator holes. Alligators continue weeding their holes until the rains return and fill the swamp once more. Although living in an alligator hole has risks for animals on the alligator's menu, it is worth the danger for creatures that would otherwise die without the benefit of their watery shelter.

Chapter 3

The Value of Swamps

Many people imagine swamps as dark and gloomy—even scary—places. For centuries, it was thought that swamps were worthless or harmful places, home only to diseases, biting insects, and dangerous animals. Because of these attitudes, swamps were often destroyed in an effort to make the land more useful to people. Even today, some people still have these same feelings about swamps.

Although many people do not realize it, swamps actually provide many benefits. Some of these benefits are easy to recognize, such as serving as a habitat for plants and animals. Some of the roles of the swamp are harder to discover. Sometimes the value of a swamp is uncovered only after it has been damaged or destroyed.

Quieting the Storm

One of the most important roles of swamps on or near the coasts of continents is to protect the land from the fury of storms. Tropical storms, hurricanes, and typhoons bring huge waves and fierce winds as they reach the shore. Swamps serve as barriers to protect inland areas from these powerful forces. Large surges of high water are absorbed by the swamp, so they cannot move farther inland and flood homes and towns.

Like many swamps, Florida's tidelands protect inland areas by acting as a buffer against severe storms.

Swamps also protect the coastal land itself. Without a swamp's network of plants that holds the soil together, even a mild storm would batter the shore. In areas where swamps have been removed, each storm that passes can cause a lot of soil to wash away. This process is called **erosion**. Erosion can happen very quickly, causing large chunks of coastal land to disappear after even just one storm.

Instead of eroding, beaches that have swamps can actually grow. The bases of the swamp plants trap sand and sediment that are pushed up onto the coast by waves. As more sand is deposited, the land grows. This creates new places for swamp plants to grow, so the process can repeat. As the coastal areas grow, more wildlife habitat is created.

A Giant Sponge

Swamps away from the coast also provide benefits during storms. When heavy rains fall and rivers flood, they overflow into nearby swamps. As the floodwaters reach the plant-filled swamps, they slow down. In areas without swamps, such as towns, the floodwaters continue to flow very fast. This can cause serious erosion and damage to property as the waters sweep quickly downstream.

Not only do swamps help slow and catch flood-water, they also help to clean it. Once slowed by the swamp, the sediment and any pollution carried in the water settles to the bottom of the swamp. Afterward, the water is much cleaner than when it entered the swamp. This purified water slowly flows through the swamp, ending up in lakes and rivers, where it may become drinking water for people. The water also may be slowly absorbed by the spongelike soil. This water eventually becomes part of the groundwater deep inside the earth.

Nature's Nursery

In addition to providing clean water for people and animals to drink, swamps also create food and shelter for wildlife. They not only provide for the creatures living within it but may also provide food for other habitats nearby. For example, some of the mangrove swamp's rich nutrients are carried out to sea by the changing tides and water currents. These nutrients provide an important food supply for beds of sea grass and coral reefs close to the shore.

Many coastal wetlands serve as areas where fish from the ocean come to breed and lay their eggs. The swamp plays an important role as a place for young fish and other aquatic animals to grow up. The young fish that hatch remain in the protected haven of the swamp until they are large enough to safely travel into the open ocean.

This is especially true in mangrove swamps. The tangled roots and rich sediments under the mangroves are ideal places for young fish, crabs, and shrimp to find shelter and food. Because there are so many places to hide in the mangroves, these young animals find protection from predators here.

The swamp provides both food and protective habitat for this Caribbean flamingo and its chick.

A shark pup swims among the mangrove roots, which protect it from larger predators.

The Swamp's Bounty

Many of the creatures that begin life in the swamp, such as shrimp, fish, crabs, and shellfish, are important food sources for people. In many coastal communities around the world, people rely heavily on catching seafood to eat and to provide a source of income. A healthy swamp where this seafood breeds and grows creates an ongoing supply of food for fishers and their families.

Many sea animals nurtured by swamps are also caught by commercial fishers. Louisiana, for example, has one of the largest fishing industries in the United States. Each year, hundreds of millions of dollars worth of seafood is taken from this state's waters. Scientists estimate that more than 75 percent of the sea creatures caught for food in Louisiana waters live in swamps and other wetlands for at least part of their lives.

Swamp Sports

Not everyone fishing in or near swamps wants to sell their catch. Recreational fishing, or fishing for sport, is very popular in many places. Some people fish in the swamps. Others fish in the waters off the coasts for the same fish caught by commercial fishers. Without swamps and other wetlands to nourish young fish, people would not have this recreational opportunity.

Swamps provide other recreation as well. Each winter millions of ducks and geese and other birds visit the swamps of southern Louisiana and Florida during their yearly **migration**. These birds attract large numbers of sport hunters. They also attract bird-watchers. Bird-watching is quickly growing in popularity all around the world. Because swamps attract a wide variety of bird species, they are popular stops for traveling bird-watchers.

People who fish, hunt, bird-watch, or participate in other recreational activities benefit from the time they spend in nature with their families. These activities also benefit the communities where they take place. Tourists spend millions of dollars on boats, equipment, guides, food, and lodging. The money from tourism keeps many small communities alive.

Swamp Tours

One of the most popular tourist activities in the swamps of Louisiana and Florida is the swamp tour. During these tours, nature guides take boatloads of visitors into a swamp to get a closer look at its unique plant and animal life. Often the animals that live in these swamps are fairly used to people and do not swim or fly away when the tour boat passes.

Bird-watchers enjoy a wide variety of bird species at the Corkscrew Swamp Sanctuary in Florida.

Tourists at Okefenokee Swamp in Georgia keep their distance from an alligator spotted during a swamp tour.

The highlight of any swamp tour is getting a glimpse of an alligator. To be sure tourists have this experience, many tour guides throw bait into the water. When the alligators hear the boat approaching, they eagerly swim toward it in anticipation of a free snack. Coming face to snout with an uncaged alligator is an experience most tourists do not soon forget! After discovering the mysterious beauty and wild creatures of the swamp, most people gain an appreciation for this special place.

Chapter 4

Swamps in Danger

Ever since European settlers arrived in the United States, people have been changing the swamp environment. At first people thought these changes would improve the quality of life for those living near swamps. More recently, however, people have come to understand that changes to swamps can have long-lasting harmful effects.

Draining and Logging Swamps

Some of the largest changes to swamps have taken place in the southeastern United States. Early settlers to Florida and Louisiana made great efforts to drain swamps and other wetlands. After removing the water with pumps or by digging canals, people could use the dry land for farming or for building homes. This effort was seen as improving the land so it could be useful to people.

Another practice that damaged swamps was logging. By the early 1900s, the enormous old-growth cypress forests of Louisiana had been almost completely cut down to meet the demand for wood. This cypress wood was prized for building homes and furniture because of its beauty and its resistance to rotting. As the cypress trees disappeared, the entire community of plants and animals in the swamp changed. One bird affected by the loss of cypress forests is the ivory-billed woodpecker. This large bird was thought to have become extinct. But in

Farmers drained the wetlands at the edge of Corkscrew Swamp in Florida to make room for this watermelon patch.

2004 scientists made several sightings of these woodpeckers in the swamps of Arkansas. The rediscovery of this species has resulted in the protection of thousands of acres of cypress forests. Scientists hope that this step will help the species to recover.

Tidal swamps in the tropics have also faced changes. For example, the mangrove trees in the coastal swamps of Southeast Asia are cleared to provide land for rice and shrimp farming and for the development of beachfront hotels.

Changing the Flow

Many other human activities, such as development to control floods and to aid boat travel through swamps, cause harm to swamps over longer periods. One area where this long-term damage continues to take place is along the Mississippi River as it flows to the sea in southern Louisiana. For millions of years, the swamps and marshes along the Mississippi served as storage areas for the enormous amounts of water that would spill over the riverbanks during the rainy season.

Today, however, people control the natural cycle of the Mississippi River's floods. Tall walls called levees have been built along the riverbanks to keep the floodwater from spilling into towns and farmland built where swamps once stood. While these levees provide protection for human property, they prevent the flow of freshwater to the remaining swamps. Without their annual flood of water and nutrients, the swamps cannot stay healthy and they dry out.

Man-made levees protect towns and farmland, but they also prevent much needed floodwater from reaching swamps.

Saltier Swamps

Without a regular flushing of freshwater from rain or floodwater, the water in swamps close to the coast becomes saltier as ocean water makes its way inland. This problem is made worse by the practice of digging canals through the swamps. These canals are dug to provide easy access for large boats traveling through the swamp from the sea. The canals are cut through the marsh grasses that normally slow the movement of seawater into the freshwater areas of the swamp.

Opening a channel in those beds of marsh grass allows salt water to flow far into the swamps with the changing tides. Plants near the coast are able to live in salty water. Plants farther upstream that are used to living in freshwater cannot. As the salty water makes its way farther upstream, the plants will die and the swamp ecosystem will eventually vanish.

Washing Away

Increasing amounts of salt water is only one problem caused by the digging of channels through swamps. The construction of canals also has led to serious erosion of soil in swamps. Canals created by people are very different from the natural channels cut by rivers and streams. Natural waterways are shallow and they twist and turn, causing the water to take a slow and curving path downstream. Canals dug by people, however, are wide and take a straight route

A boat travels through a canal at the Okefenokee Swamp in Florida, the largest swamp in North America.

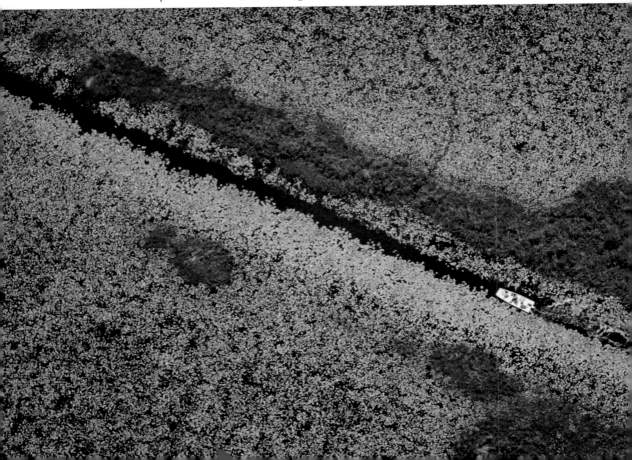

through the swamp. Water flows very quickly in these deep channels. Large boats traveling through the canals create sizable waves that hit the shore.

As a result of people's actions, the shore along the canals is very unstable. When the canals were dug, large piles of mud were scooped from the water and mounded along the canal's edges. This mud covered and destroyed the plants growing on the banks of the canal. Without plants to hold the soil together, the fast-moving water and waves in the canals cause the soil to constantly wash away and the land to erode. This, in turn, causes the canal to grow ever wider and deeper.

Swamp Invaders

Erosion is a serious problem in swamps, but so are aliens. These aliens are plants that are not part of the natural landscape of the swamp and usually come from other countries. Known as exotics or nonnatives, these plants have been brought to the swamp by people. Sometimes people plant them on purpose for their gardens or as a farming crop. Other times they are accidentally brought to the swamp after hitchhiking on boats or in the soil of imported plants.

As birds or the wind spread the seeds of exotics, the plants take root throughout the swamp. In their new environment exotic plants do not face the natural insect enemies and diseases that can damage or kill them at home. Without the controls that keep them in check in their natural habitat, these plants

Water hyacinths are lovely to look at, but these invasive plants quickly choke other plants out of swamps and ponds.

can multiply rapidly and cover large areas. When this happens, these plants are called **invasive**.

Invasive plants are trouble for the native plants and animals of a swamp. They can grow so fast that they choke out the other plants. Animals that rely on native plants for food and shelter may disappear when exotics take over. In some Florida swamps the invasive plants water hyacinth and hydrilla grow so thick in the water in some areas that fish are forced out and people can no longer boat or swim. The melaleuca tree and the Brazilian pepper tree have invaded tens of thousands of acres (hectares) in the

Everglades in southern Florida, squeezing out native trees that once stood in their place.

Swamp Loss

Invasive plants, erosion, the construction of levees and canals, draining, and logging all have resulted in major changes to swamps and other wetlands. In fact, wetlands are at serious risk all over the world. In the Sundarbans, as much as half of the mangrove forests has been destroyed. In the Philippines, 75 percent of the mangrove swamps has been removed in the last 60 years.

In the United States, more than half of the nation's wetlands—more than 100 million acres (40

A victim of industrialization, a mangrove swamp in Malaysia is cleared away.

million hectares)—has disappeared due to development and logging activity. Nowhere is this problem more serious than in Louisiana. Louisiana's wetlands are dying. This is mostly due to the changes that have been made to the natural flow of the Mississippi River.

For the last 50 years, Louisiana has been losing land at the rate of 34 square miles (54 sq. km) each year. Most of this land is the swampland and marshes along Louisiana's coast. If the problem continues, scientists estimate that by 2050 the shoreline will be 33 miles (53km) farther inland than it is today.

Turning the Tide

Faced with these numbers, many people are now calling for changes to protect swamps. Louisiana is developing a large-scale program to recreate wetlands and slow erosion. In Thailand, the government provides money to rehabilitate mangrove swamps. In Indonesia, new laws are in place to prevent the removal of mangrove trees.

These actions demonstrate what will likely be the most important step in saving swamps—a change in attitude. As people learn how healthy swamps benefit both people and wildlife, they will support efforts to protect this unique and fragile ecosystem.

Glossary

aquatic: Relating to or living in the water.

buttress roots: Roots that flare out from the base of a tree to provide support.

ecosystem: The connected network of plants, animals, and weather systems that make up a specific pocket of nature.

epiphytes: Plants that grow on another plant, receiving moisture and nutrients from the air and rain instead of the soil.

erosion: The wearing away of soil from the action of water, wind, or rain.

hydric: Full of water.

hydrophytic: Growing in water.

invasive: Tending to spread rapidly and aggressively.

migration: To move from one climate or region to another.

pneumatophores: Roots of a mangrove plant that extend out of the ground to absorb oxygen from the air.

sediments: Soil and other solid material carried downstream by rivers.

stilt roots: Roots that extend from the trunks of mangrove trees and provide support. Also known as prop roots.

For Further Exploration

Books

Richard Beatty, *Biomes Atlases: Wetlands.* Austin, TX: Steck-Vaughn, 2002. This well-illustrated volume provides great information on the ecology and conservation needs of wetlands. Specific wetlands are profiled, including the Sundarbans of India and Bangladesh.

Rebecca L. Johnson, *A Journey into a Wetland.* Minneapolis: Carolrhoda, 2004. Illustrated with photographs and drawings, this book offers a glimpse into a day in the life of an alligator and the other swamp creatures it encounters.

Bianca Lavies, *Mangrove Wilderness.* New York: Dutton Children's Books, 1994. This book gives a detailed account of Florida's mangrove ecosystem, including the unique life cycle of this coastal plant.

Melissa Stewart, *Life in a Wetland.* Minneapolis: Lerner, 2003. This book provides an overview of the types of wetlands that make up the ecosystem of southern Florida's Everglades region. It also describes the role that humans have played in changing the natural balance of the Everglades and how conservation efforts will shape its future.

Web Sites
The Everglades Ecosystem
(www.nps.gov/ever/eco). This National Park Service Web site offers a wealth of information on the variety of wetland habitats and the wildlife of the Florida Everglades.

U.S. Environmental Protection Agency
(www.epa.gov/OWOW/wetlands/vital/toc.html). This site contains information on types of wetlands, wildlife of the wetlands, and the benefits wetlands provide to people.

Index

Picture Credits

Cover: James L. Amos/CORBIS

America 24-7/Getty Images, 14

© Bill Banaszewski/Visuals Unlimited, 38

Corel Corp., 10, 15 (upper right), 24, 38 (inset)

© David Muench/CORBIS, 9, 17

© Douglas Peebles/CORBIS, 12

Farrell Grehan/National Geographic/Getty
    Images, 5

Jim Wark/Lonely Planet Images, 36

Lee Foster/Lonely Planet Images, 31

© Marty Snyderman/Visuals Unlimited, 28

Photodisc, 20 (center, upper left, upper right)

Photos.com, 15 (all except upper right), 20 (lower
    left, lower right)

© Raymond Gehman/CORBIS, 30, 33

© Roy Toft/National Geographic/Getty Images, 6

© Sally A. Morgan; Ecoscene/CORBIS, 39

© Steve Winter/National Geographic/Getty
    Images, 27

Terry McTigue, ORR/NOS/NOAA, 35

© Theo Allofs/CORBIS, 18

About the Author

Karen D. Povey has spent her career as a conservation educator, working to instill an appreciation for wildlife in people of all ages. Karen makes her home in Tacoma, Washington, where she presents live-animal education programs at Point Defiance Zoo & Aquarium.